Kids on Earth

A Children's Documentary Series Exploring Global Cultures & The Natural World

PORTUGAL

By Sensei Paul David

COPYRIGHT PAGE

Kids on Earth: A Children's Documentary Series Exploring
Global Cultures & The Natural World - Portugal
by Sensei Paul David,

978-1-77848-071-3 KoE_PORTUGAL_Ingram_HardBackBook Hardcover

978-1-77848-070-6 KoE_PORTUGAL_Ingram_PaperBackBook

978-1-77848-069-0 KoE_PORTUGAL_Amazon_PaperbackBook

978-1-77848-068-3 KoE_PORTUGAL_Amazon_eBook

www.senseipublishing.com

@senseipublishing
#senseipublishing

Get Our FREE Books Now!

lifeofbailey.senseipublishing.com

kidsonearth.senseipublishing.com

Click Below or Search Amazon for Another Book In Each Series Or Visit:

www.amazon.com/author/senseipauldavid

Join Our Publishing Journey!

If you would like to receive FUTURE FREE BOOKS and get to know us better, please click www.senseipublishing.com and join our newsletter by entering your email address in the pop-up box.

Follow Our Blog: senseipauldavid.ca

Follow/Like/Subscribe: Facebook, Instagram, YouTube: @senseipublishing

Scan the QR Code with your phone or tablet to follow us on social media:

Like / Subscribe / Follow

Olá everybody! Welcome to the Portuguese Republic! My name is Sofia, and this is my brother Rodrigo. We are from a beautiful country in Europe called Portugal. Have you heard of it?

Portugal is a small country in Western Europe. It is one of the oldest nations in Europe.

We are so excited to show you around our historic and beautiful country. Grab your family, and let's go on an adventure. Are you ready to explore the ancient castles, busy cities, and calming beaches of Portugal?

FUN FACTS

Portugal is 868 square miles big. That makes it almost the same size as the American state of Indiana.

We only have one neighbouring country. This country is called Spain.

Portugal has a long coastline along the Atlantic Ocean. There are many beautiful beaches and scenic cliffs here!

Our flag is red and green, with our national coat of arms in the middle. The green symbolizes hope for the future, and the red remembers the pain of the past. The Portuguese flag was first designed in 1910. That means it is over 100 years old!

There are three main cities here in Portugal. The biggest city is also our capital. It is called Lisbon, and it is one of the most wonderful cities in the world. We live here in Lisbon, along with about 5,18,000 other people.

Porto is one of the biggest cities in northern Portugal. It is a medieval city that is almost 900 years old! In fact, Portugal was named after this ancient city.

The most southern city in Portugal is called Faro. Not too many people live here, but it is a very popular place for tourists to visit. People love to visit Faro for its fantastic beaches and warm sunshine!

FUN FACTS

Lisbon is the westernmost city in Europe and the oldest city on the European continent. Our home city is over 2700 years old!

There are many important Portuguese landmarks here in Lisbon, including the Belem Tower and the Jeronimos Monastery. Follow along if you would like to learn more!

Did you know that the city of Faro was almost destroyed by earthquakes in the 1700s?

Because Portugal is on the Atlantic Ocean and near to the Mediterranean Sea, it has both a Mediterranean and an Atlantic climate.

We have a mild climate in Portugal. Our summers are warm and dry, with a lot of sunshine and very little rain. When winter comes, the weather can get cold, rainy, and windy. The weather is always cooler by the ocean and warmer in the middle of the country.

Because we live in the Northern Hemisphere, our winter starts in December and ends in February, and our summer is from June to September.

The warmest month in Lisbon is August. Most days, the temperature is around 74 degrees Fahrenheit.

FUN FACTS

High up in the Estrela Mountains, it can get as cold as 32 degrees Fahrenheit. We like to visit the Estrela Mountains to go skiing during winter!

A small town called Amareleja near the Spanish border is one of the hottest places in Europe. It once reached 117 degrees Fahrenheit here. That sounds too hot to handle!

Do you want to know something special about Portugal? Portugal also includes two archipelagos in the middle of the Atlantic Ocean. These archipelagos are called the Madeira Islands and the Azores, and they are beautiful islands to visit.

Madeira has eight islands, but people only live on two of these islands. They are called Madeira Island and Porto Santo. The other six rocky islands are home to only wild goats and rabbits.

There are nine islands in the Azores. The largest city here is called Ponta Delgada. Many tourists visit the Azores for its beautiful beaches and five-star hotels.

FUN FACTS

An archipelago is a group of many islands found in the ocean. The Azores and Madeira were created when underwater volcanoes erupted millions of years ago.

Madeira Island is only 34 miles long. Porto Santo is even smaller. It only takes about one hour and forty minutes to fly from Lisbon to Madeira, and two and a half hours from Lisbon to the Azores.

Both Madeira and the Azores are autonomous regions. This means that even though they are part of Portugal, they have their own local governments.

Azores
Madeira
Atlantic Ocean

10.31 million people are living in Portugal. Compared to other European countries, we don't have such a big population.

Only about 250000 people live in the Madeira Islands. Every year, over 1.5 million people travel to these islands as tourists. This means there are more tourists here than there are locals!

The city of Porto is home to about 249663 people. One-third of the Portuguese population live in Lisbon and Porto. The other two-thirds live along the long Atlantic coastline. Only a small portion of our people live inland in small farming villages.

FUN FACTS

0.13% of the world's population lives in Portugal. How cool is that!

Scientists predict our population will get even smaller in the future.

Porto
249,663 people
Lisbon
544,851 people
MADEIRA ISLANDS

Portugal is very special because of the ancient cultures and traditions we still follow today. Some people think we have a similar way of life to other Mediterranean countries like Spain and France.

Everyone in Portugal values spending time with their families. We like to eat meals with our families and help each other out whenever we can. We are very loyal to our families and friends, and we believe that trust and respect are very important.

FUN FACTS

The Portuguese have a big café culture. As you can imagine, this means that all through the day and the night, you can find our older siblings and parents sipping coffee in street cafés and chatting with their friends.

CAFÉ

More than 81% of people in Portugal follow the Roman Catholic religion. This is a style of Christianity that was brought to the country when Portugal was part of the Roman Empire.

Like other Christian religions, Catholics believe in the Holy Bible. We believe that Jesus was the son of God and that his mother Mary was a very holy person. We pray to our God in a church. What religion do you follow?

Roman Catholicism has helped create the country that we live in today, from the culture and traditions we follow to the beliefs we have and the festivals we celebrate. This religion has even shaped how we spend time with our friends and family, and how our government works.

FUN FACTS

Every village, town, and city in Portugal has at least one church. Many of these churches were built hundreds of years ago as the center of each town.

One of the oldest churches in Portugal is called the Cathedral of Saint Mary Major, and it is right here in our home city of Lisbon! It was built in 1147. Can you believe that this church is almost 1000 years old?

Our parents tell us lots of interesting mythical bedtime stories that have been passed down from our ancestors. My favourite story is about the Moutas Encantadas. These are apparently magical creatures that look after the bridges, castles, caves, and rivers in Portugal.

Most of our traditions and values come from our Christian history. We always respect our elders here. I look up to my mother and father for help when I need it. Here in Portugal, older people always dress respectfully and beautifully. This is a way of showing that they are successful.

Rodrigo and I were taught how to eat with good manners. We only start to eat once our mother says 'bom apetite.' This means 'enjoy your meal' in Portuguese. We eat with a knife and fork and keep our elbows off the table. Do you know how to eat with good manners?

FUN FACTS

If you visit us for dinner, our parents like it when guests bring a small gift. Whatever you do, don't give my mother 13 flowers. This is because the number 13 is unlucky in Portugal!

Portugal is one of the most formal and conservative countries in Europe. Being conservative means being very traditional and respectful of others.

Would you like to see the national clothing of Portugal? Our national clothing is very bright and colourful.

On special occasions like weddings and festivals, our mother wears a bouffant skirt made from a checkered red or white material called the saia. Women wear the saia with a white linen shirt and sometimes a tight waistcoat. The final touch is a decorative apron embroidered with flowers in many colours. I can't wait to get my own bouffant skirt when I am older!

Our father wears short pants which are tightly gathered just below his knees, a wide-brimmed sombrero hat, and a waistcoat.

FUN FACTS

When you visit Rodrigo and me in Portugal, you might notice that we wear modern clothing just like you. Even though we wear western outfits, we like to dress conservatively and look formal every day.

A Portuguese kerchief is a small scarf or bandana which some women wear around their heads.

Most of the traditional clothing in Portugal is modest and formal. The type of traditional clothing you wear depends on the region you are from.

You won't believe how unique the history of our country is. People have been living on the Iberian Peninsula for thousands of years. The first people who lived here were called the Iberians. They lived in Portugal in the 1st century.

In the 2nd century, the Roman Empire took control of Iberia. They ruled over our land for over six centuries, spreading their Catholic religion, culture, and traditions across Portugal.

FUN FACTS

The Iberian Peninsula is the piece of land that today includes the countries of Portugal and Spain.

The Roman Empire was the largest empire of the ancient world. Its capital was in Rome, and the empire ruled across many Mediterranean countries.

If we go back even further, scientists believe that neanderthals lived in Portugal over 40000 years ago. Neanderthals were a type of primate that looked similar to humans.

THE ROMAN EMPIRE
THE IBERIAN PENINSULA

In the 16th Century, European nations began exploring the world by boat. When they landed in different places, they believed that they had found new countries and taken control over land that was not theirs. This time was known as the period of colonialism.

Portugal's location on the Atlantic Ocean gave our ancestors an advantage when exploring the oceans. Two explorers named Vasco da Gama and Bartolomeu Dias were the first to travel around the African continent. They became very famous for their ocean exploration!

Portugal colonized many African, South American, and Asian countries. This is how the Portuguese language spread across the world.

FUN FACTS

Vasco da Gama was a famous Portuguese explorer who found a route around the African continent to help Portugal trade with Asia. Can you imagine sailing through waters that had never been explored before?

Colonization is when one country takes control over another. Countries would colonize other places to steal their money and take control of their natural resources. This was a terrible time for the colonized countries in Africa, South America and Asia.

Portugal's colonies were a part of the Portuguese Empire. This empire was 23 times bigger than the size of the Portuguese homeland.

DOM VASCO DA GAM
1469 - 1524
DESCOBRIDOR E ALMIRANTE DO MAR DA IND
CONDE DA VIDIGUEIRA
VICE-REI DA INDIA

We have many national monuments here in Portugal. The most famous monument is called the Tower of Belem. It is a fort that used to be the gateway to the city of Lisbon. Today, you can climb to the top of a spiral staircase and see beautiful city views from the tower rooftop.

The Jeronimos Monastery is another important monument. It was built to remember the boat trip that Vasco da Gama took around the world.

FUN FACTS

The Tower of Belem was built between 1514 and 1520. It is a UNESCO World Heritage Site.

Portugal has 17 different UNESCO World Heritage Sites. That is a lot for such a small country! In fact, there are another 19 sites that might be added to the list soon.

Our ancestors started to build the Jeronimos Monastery in 1501, but the building was only finished over 200 years later in the 1700s!

THE TOWER OF BELEM

Have you ever visited a medieval fortress? One of my favourite places to visit is the town of Sintra. There are many different castles, palaces, and fortresses here, but my favourite is the yellow, blue, red, and purple coloured Pena Palace. Rodrigo thinks this palace looks like it could be in Disney Land!

The Castle of the Moors is a medieval fortress built in the 8th and 9th centuries. It was built on top of a hill overlooking Sintra, to protect the farmlands and people from attacks. Today, you can still walk along the fortress's walls.

FUN FACTS

Sintra is a region in Portugal, a few hours drive from Lisbon. This historic center is known for its beautiful palaces, ancient fortress ruins, and fancy estates and gardens.

The whole region of Sintra is a UNESCO World Heritage Site!

Can you guess what language we speak in Portugal? You guessed it! Portuguese is the official national language of Portugal.

Our national language spread across the world when our ancestors explored and colonized countries in Africa, South America, and Asia. Not only is Portuguese the fourth most spoken language in the world, but it is also the national language of nine different countries.

FUN FACTS

The Portuguese language that we speak today came from Latin and Galician languages that were spoken on the Iberian Peninsula many centuries ago.

Galician languages are dialects that were spoken in the region of Galicia in Northern Portugal.

The longest Portuguese word has 29 letters! Can you imagine writing out such a long word?

Did you know that only 5% of Portuguese speakers live in Portugal? It is spoken by over 215 million people worldwide and is the most common language in South America.

Portuguese is the second-fastest-growing European language in the world, behind English.

Portuguese
Aqui falamos
português

When you visit Rodrigo and me in Portugal, you should try to learn some basic words and phrases in Portuguese:

- **Olá** - Hello
- **Tchau** - Bye
- **Tudo bem**? - How are you?
- **Por favor** - Please
- **Obrigado/Obrigada** - Thank you
- **De nada** - You are welcome
- **Prazer** - Nice to meet you

If you don't understand what someone is saying, try saying **'Alguém aqui fala inglês?'**. This translates to 'Does anyone here speak English?'

Most people in Lisbon and Porto can understand English, but only 27% of the Portuguese population speak English. Our people always appreciate it when tourists take the time to learn our language.

FUN FACTS

Did you know that the Portuguese that our friends speak in Brazil is slightly different from how Rodrigo and I speak in Portugal?

Spanish is another language that was born from Galician and Latin. This is why you might find many words that sound similar in Portuguese and Spanish.

Olá - Hello
Tchau - Bye
Tudo bem? - How are you?
Por favor - Please
Obrigado/Obrigada - Thank you
De nada - You are welcome
Prazer - Nice to meet you

The Portuguese Empire used to be the world's richest empire. When we granted our colonies independence in the 19th century, our country became one of the poorest in Western Europe.

Today, many of our friend's parents work in offices in the big cities. In smaller villages, people work on farms or in vineyards.

Have you heard of renewable energy? Renewable energy is when countries use energy from the sun, water, and wind to make electricity. Portugal is one of the world's leaders in renewable energy, and many people have jobs working to create clean energy for our cities.

When we go shopping, we pay using the Euro. This is a currency used by all the countries that are part of the European Union.

FUN FACTS

A vineyard is a type of farm that grows grapes to make wine. Portugal makes some of the best sweet wines in Europe. These wines are called port. Adults usually drink port when they eat dessert.

Tourism is another important economic sector here. Many people work in restaurants, hotels, or as tour guides.

We are lucky to live in a country with a low unemployment rate. This means that most Portuguese adults have jobs.

Until 1999, we used to use our own Portuguese currency called the Escudo.

A long time ago, Portugal used to have a royal family known as the Portuguese Monarchy. When the monarchy was overthrown in 1910, Portugal became a republic with a government.

Since 1976, we have had a presidential-representative democracy. This means that our people vote for a new president every five years in a democratic election. The government is guided by the prime minister, who is elected every four years.

Our home joined the European Union in 1986. This helped our economy grow strong and improved the way we live today.

FUN FACTS

A democratic election is when the people of a country vote for who they want as a government. Each person over the age of 18 has a voice and a vote.

The European Union is an organization that was created to bring European countries together so that they can make the continent a better place for everyone who lives there.

We love to eat delicious seafood here. You might have heard of the codfish. We call this Bacalhau, and it is our national food. We dry and salt the fish before soaking it in milk and cooking it.

Rodrigo's favourite food is Piri-Piri chicken! Piri-Piri is a spicy sauce cooked with chicken on an open fire. This sauce was first made by our ancestors when they colonized the African country of Mozambique.

Our parents use a lot of olive oil, tomato, and spices when they cook. Almost every meal is a fish or a meat dish with a side of rice, beans, bread, or vegetables.

If you visit us in Portugal, make sure you try a Pasteis de Nata. These are tasty sweet custard tarts that you can buy from almost any bakery or market!

FUN FACTS

Did you know that over one-third of our land is used for farming? That is a lot of space!

Our families grow a lot of organic food. Organic farming is when we farm without using dangerous chemicals and pesticides to get rid of bugs and pests. This makes our food very delicious and nutritious!

Even though the country is small, Portugal has a very diverse geography. The Tagus River runs across the country, from Spain to the Atlantic Ocean, and cuts Portugal into two halves.

There are many mountains in the north of the country. Rodrigo and I like to ski in the Estrela Mountains with our family in winter. These mountains are 6500 feet high.

If you travel south of the Tagus River, you will find many rolling hills and flat plains. In the very south of Portugal, there is a beautiful region known as the Algarve. This place is known for its picture-perfect fishing villages, dramatic cliff faces, and sandy beaches. No wonder there are always so many tourists here!

FUN FACTS

The highest Portuguese mountain peak is on Ilha do Pico Island in the Azores. This mountain is 7713 feet high.

The Tagus River runs 170 miles through Portugal!

Because Portugal sits between Europe, Africa, the Mediterranean Sea, and the Atlantic Ocean, our country has many different landscapes. You can find shrublands, grasslands, sand dunes, coastal cliffs, lagoons, and of course, long coastlines.

Mainland Portugal is home to over 3600 different types of plants. I think you might have heard of our national flower. It is called Lavender! There are about 30 different species of lavender here in Portugal. You can also find lots of fresh herbs and other delicious-smelling flowers growing wild in our country.

The Azores and Madeira Islands are home to some unique plants. The volcanoes that created these islands made some of the most fertile soil in the world. Today, you can find tons of colourful hydrangeas growing wild on the islands!

FUN FACTS

Did you know that one-third of the world's cork forests are in Portugal? We produce over half of the world's cork wood right here in our country! Cork is a type of light wood used to close wine bottles.

Hydrangeas are beautiful flowers that have many small flowers connected to one head. A single hydrangea flower can look like a bunch of flowers!

We need to work together to protect our wild plants and animals from losing their natural habitat. Do you have any great ideas to help keep our plants safe?

LAVENDER
CORK TREE
HYDRANGEAS

A long time ago, our home used to be one huge forest. Today, most of the land in Portugal has been turned into cities and farmland, but there are still a few areas where wild animals can run free.

Only one-quarter of our forests are still standing today. In these forests, there are many boars, deer, foxes, wild goats, and Iberian hares.

The Iberian Lynx is the most extraordinary wild animal living in Portugal. It is endemic to the Iberian Peninsula. Unfortunately, it is also the most endangered cat species in the world.

FUN FACTS

When an animal is endemic, it means that it only lives in one area. This makes the Iberian Lynx a special animal that we should protect. We are working with our neighbours in Spain to make space for the Iberian lynxes to run freely.

Endangered animals are close to dying out on earth because they have lost their homes, food or have been hunted.

Iberian Lynx

There aren't so many lizards and snakes slithering around the Portuguese wilderness. In Lisbon, we don't see any reptiles crawling around at all.

The southern Algarve is scattered with beautiful butterflies and moths. You will also see a lot of flies and beetles around the country.

The Portuguese millipede is a small creature that likes to crawl into our homes. They look a bit creepy, but they can't hurt us!

FUN FACTS

Portugal only has 25 different reptile species. There are two dangerous snakes in Portugal, but they like to hide from humans.

Can you believe that Portuguese millipedes were first found in Australia? I wonder why they aren't named Australian millipedes instead? They can live for over two years!

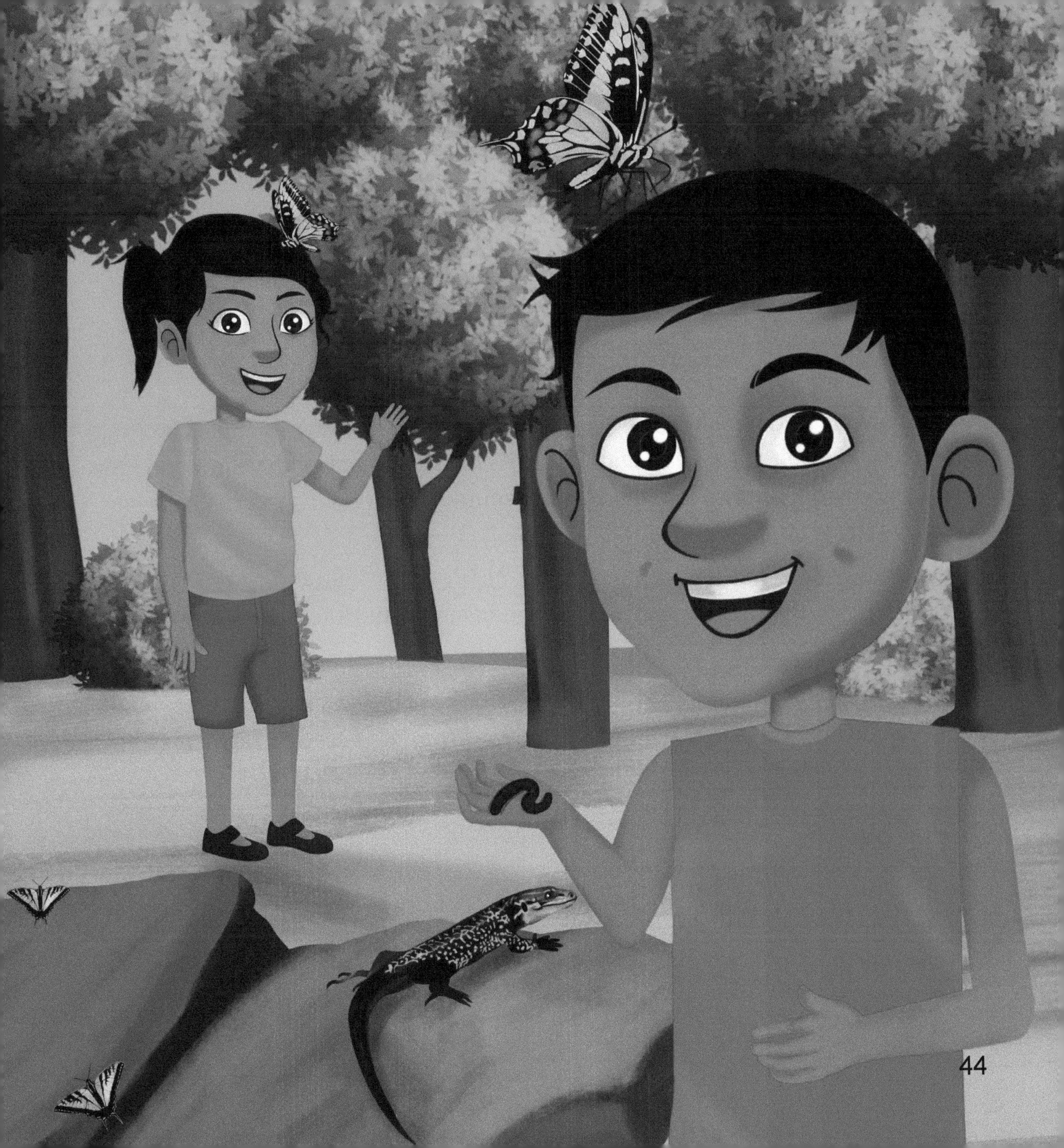

Would you like to meet some Portuguese birds? Most birds live around the wetlands in northern Portugal and around the Tagus River.

Three endemic birds live in Portugal, but they all live on the Azores and Madeira Islands. The Madeira Firecrest is our favourite bird. It is small with yellow and grey feathers. Rodrigo thinks it looks like a tiny tennis ball!

FUN FACTS

We have 626 different bird species living on the mainland, the Azores and Madeira Islands.

During the summer months, many migratory birds land in Portugal on their journey between Europe and Africa. Migratory birds fly from the Northern Hemisphere to the Southern Hemisphere every year to follow summer. Isn't that amazing!

MADEIRA FIRECREST
GREY HERON
NORTHERN FLICKER

With such a long coastline, you can only imagine the exciting sea life that lives below the water! Tuna, bonito, and sardines are the most common fish along our coastline. Many fishermen sail into the water to catch these fish.

There are also a lot of crabs, clams, lobster, and oysters along the Portuguese coastline. Oysters are my favourite food to eat. Have you ever tried an oyster?

Turtles are very common in our seas. The loggerhead turtle is a giant turtle that can weigh up to 300 pounds! If you're very lucky, you might see an Atlantic ridley sea turtle. Not only is this turtle endangered, but it is also the rarest turtle species in the world.

FUN FACTS

Eight different turtle species are swimming in the Portuguese seas.

We also have many sharks living here. Most of them are not so dangerous. You can find blue sharks and mako sharks in our waters.

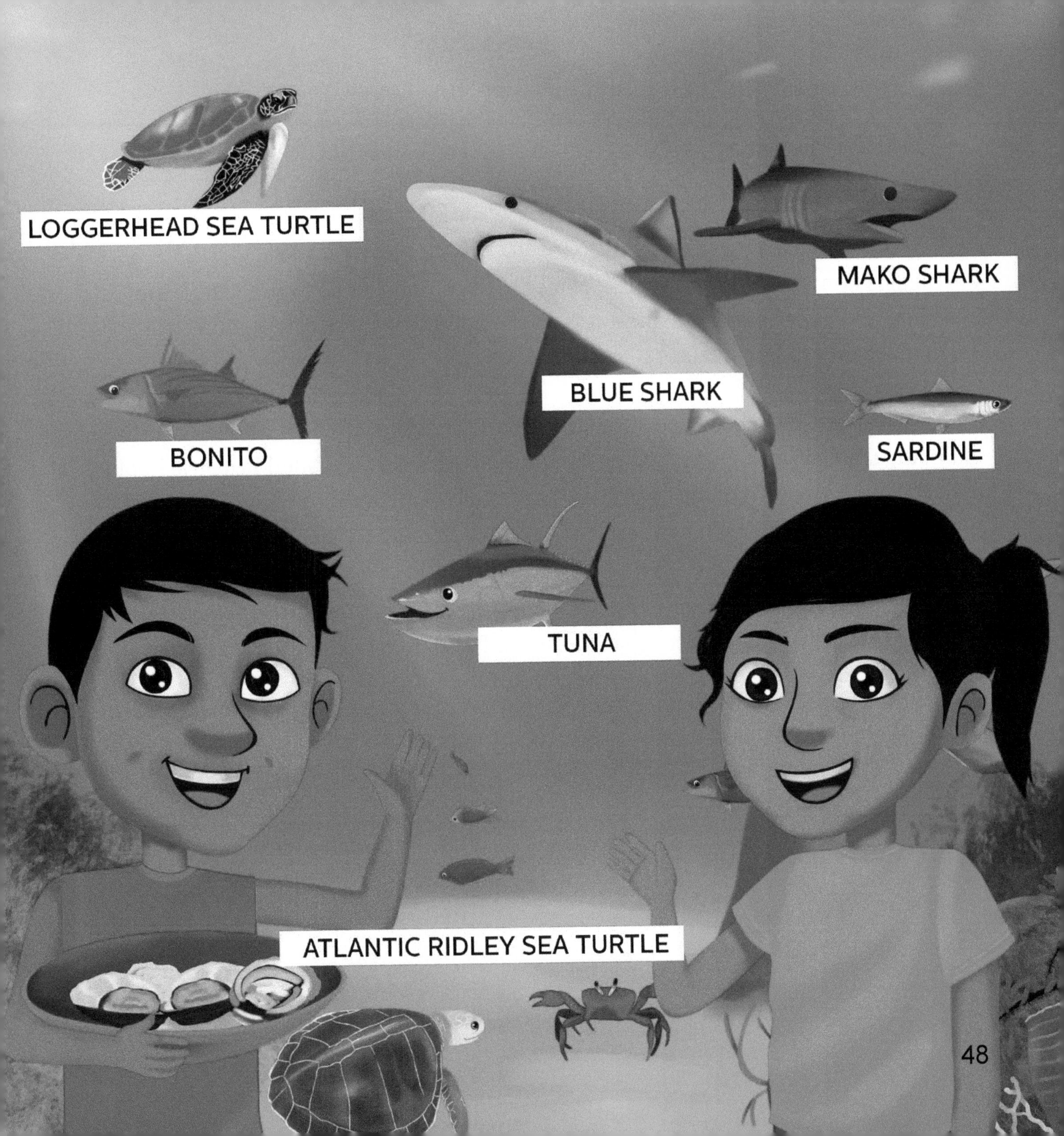
LOGGERHEAD SEA TURTLE
MAKO SHARK
BLUE SHARK
BONITO
SARDINE
TUNA
ATLANTIC RIDLEY SEA TURTLE

Portugal is known as one of the best places to surf in the world. With such a long coastline and year-round sunshine, it is no surprise that there are so many great surfing beaches in Portugal.

Some of the world's most important surfing competitions are held on the Atlantic coast of Portugal every year. One of the best spots to surf is a town called Ericeira. Peniche is a local fishing village that also has great waves.

FUN FACTS

Did you know that you can find one of the world's best big-wave surf spots in Portugal? Professional surfers visit Nazaré in Praia do Norte to surf massive waves.

The waves here are often higher than 65 feet tall. The biggest wave ever surfed at Nazaré was higher than 80 feet. Can you imagine a massive wall of water breaking in the ocean? You need to have special safety equipment and be a professionally trained surfer to surf here.

Wherever you go in Portugal, you will see buildings decorated with beautifully painted blue and white tiles. These ceramic tiles are called azulejos. They cover the walls of train stations, famous buildings, restaurants, and churches.

Azulejos is a special tile glazing art that is a big part of our Portuguese culture. These tiles are painted with pictures that tell the stories of our history.

The oldest tiles show the history of Portuguese explorers sailing the seas on famous ships called the caravel. Modern tile art shows animals and beautiful decorative patterns in blue and white colours.

FUN FACTS

You can see azulejos tiles just about everywhere in Lisbon. We love to look at the different tiles on the walls when we walk near our house.

The most historic tile art was painted in the 15th century. There are many museums where you can admire the old azulejos tiles.

We love to sing and dance in Portugal. Almost every small town has its own ‘terreiro’, which means ‘dance floor’ in English. Each region of the country has its own traditional dance styles and songs.

The national dance of Portugal is called the vira. It is a traditional dance that is most common in north Portugal. The vira has a three-step rhythm and is danced very fast.

Fado is the traditional music that you will hear across the country. Rodrigo thinks it sounds a bit sad.

FUN FACTS

Fado is Portuguese folk music that became popular in the 1800s.

Fado singers are known as fadistas. They sing about how hard life can be, but also about our hopes and dreams. Fadistas wear a black coat when they sing Fado.

Sport is an important part of Portuguese culture. Bullfighting is an old tradition that is still played in a suburb called Vila Franca da Xira in Lisbon. In this game, a player rides a horse and tries to make a big bull charge at them.

Like many other western European countries, football is the most popular sport in Portugal. Did you know that some of the world's most famous football players are from our country? You might have heard of Christiano Ronaldo before. He is from the Madeira Islands!

Some of the best golf courses in Europe can be found around the Algarve and Estoril coast. Every year, the world's top golfers come to the Algarve to compete in the Algarve Portugal Open.

FUN FACTS

There are three huge stadiums here that can seat over 50000 people.
Estádio da Luz is the biggest stadium. It is located right here in our home city of Lisbon. 64642 people can fit into this stadium!

Our home football team is the most supported football club in the world! It is called the Lisboa e Benfica. 'Lisboa' is how we say 'Lisbon' in Portuguese.

Many people like to spend time outdoors in nature. Cycling, hiking, sailing, and surfing are other sports that our friends love to do.

Rodrigo and I love to learn. We go to school five days a week just like you do!

One of the best things about Portugal is that most kids go to school to get a good education. This way, we can all grow up to be successful adults with good jobs.

Rodrigo wants to be a doctor when he is older. What do you want to do when you grow up?

FUN FACTS

Portugal has a high literacy rate. Over 90% of the people who live here can read and write.

Every child between the age of six and fifteen has to go to school. Once we have finished twelve years of school, there are many different universities and colleges where we can go to learn even more!

ESPANHA
ESPANHA

We had such a great time showing you around our exciting home country. We have so much more to share with you, and we hope you can come and visit us in Portugal one day soon!

We have a long history of famous explorers and royal kings.
Our culture is rich, and traditions are important to us.
We eat tasty food that comes from our land and sea.
Some beautiful endangered animals live here in Portugal.
We love to play sports and spend time outdoors.
We value each other and enjoy spending time with our families.

We are proud of our people for taking care of our environment. It makes us happy to live in a place where we can get a good education and learn interesting things.

We hope you enjoyed learning about our country, animals, people and traditions as much as we loved teaching you.

Obrigada!

Visit us at www.senseipublishing.com and sign up for our newsletter to learn more about our exciting books and to experience our **FREE Guided Meditations for Kids & Adults**.

As always...

It's a great day to be alive!

What have you learned about Portugal?

Take this quiz to see how much you have learned about Sofia and Rodrigo's home country!

1) What is the capital city of Portugal called?
    a) Porto
    b) Lisbon
    c) Ericeira
    d) Faro

2) What ocean does Portugal lie on?
    a) The Black Sea
    b) The Mediterranean Sea
    c) The Atlantic Ocean
    d) The Indian Ocean

3) What religion does 81% of the Portuguese people follow?
    a) Islam
    b) Roman Catholicism
    c) Christianity
    d) Hinduism

4) How many countries speak Portuguese as their national language?
    a) 1
    b) 7
    c) 5
    d) 9

5) What cat species is endemic to Portugal? (Hint: it is also endangered)
   a) Lion
   b) Tiger
   c) Iberian Lynx
   d) Panther

6) What currency do the Portuguese use today?
   a) The Portuguese
   b) The Euro

7) What is the national food of Portugal?
   a) Bacalhau
   b) Pasteis de Nata
   c) Piri-Piri chicken
   d) Sardines

8) BONUS QUESTION: Can you name the two island archipelagos that are part of Portugal?

   ____

Don't forget to share all of the new things you have learned with a friend!

Answers: 1-b, 2-c, 3-b, 4-d, 5-c, 6-b, 7-a

Thank you for reading this book!

If you found this book helpful, I would be grateful if you would **post an honest review on Amazon** so this book can reach other supportive readers like you!

All you need to do is digitally flip to the back and leave your review. Or visit amazon.com/author/senseipauldavid click the correct book cover and click on the blue link next to the yellow stars that say, "customer reviews."

As always...

It's a great day to be alive!

Get/Share Our FREE All-Ages Mental Health Books Now!

lifeofbailey.senseipublishing.com

kidsonearth.senseipublishing.com

Click Below or Search Amazon for Another Book In Each Series Or Visit:

www.amazon.com/author/senseipauldavid

@senseipublishing
#senseipublishing

Check out our **recommendations** for other books for adults & kids plus other great resources by visiting www.senseipublishing.com/resources/

Join Our Publishing Journey!

If you would like to receive FREE BOOKS, special offers, please visit www.senseipublishing.com and join our newsletter by entering your email address in the pop-up box

Follow Our Engaging Blog NOW! senseipauldavid.ca

Get Our FREE Books Today!

Click & Share the Links Below

FREE Kids Books

lifeofbailey.senseipublishing.com
kidsonearth.senseipublishing.com

FREE Self-Development Book

senseiselfdevelopment.senseipublishing.com

FREE BONUS!!!

Experience Over 25 FREE Engaging Guided Meditations!

Prized Skills & Practices for Adults & Kids. Help Restore Deep-Sleep, Lower Stress, Improve Posture, Navigate Uncertainty & More.

Download the Free Insight Timer App and click the link below:
http://insig.ht/sensei_paul

About Sensei Publishing

Sensei Publishing commits itself to helping people of all ages transform into better versions of themselves by providing high-quality and research-based self-development books with an emphasis on mental health and guided meditations. Sensei Publishing offers well-written e-books, audiobooks, paperbacks and online courses that simplify complicated but practical topics in line with its mission to inspire people towards positive transformation.

It's a great day to be alive!

About the Author

I create simple & transformative eBooks & Guided Meditations for Adults & Children proven to help navigate uncertainty, solve niche problems & bring families closer together.

I'm a former finance project manager, private pilot, jiu-jitsu instructor, musician & former University of Toronto Fitness Trainer. I prefer a science-based approach to focus on these & other areas in my life to stay humble & hungry to evolve. I hope you enjoy my work and I'd love to hear your feedback.

- It's a great day to be alive!
Sensei Paul David

Scan & Follow/Like/Subscribe: Facebook, Instagram, YouTube: @senseipublishing

Scan using your phone/iPad camera for Social Media
Visit us at www.senseipublishing.com and sign up for our newsletter to learn more about our exciting books and to experience our FREE Guided Meditations for Kids & Adults.

Ingram Content Group UK Ltd.
Milton Keynes UK
UKHW051602180723
425309UK00014B/62

9 781778 480706